Mozart the Clinic Cat

THE CHRISTMAS VET

by Delicia Miller

illustrated by Maxine Kuepfer

ISBN: 978-1-990336-59-1
Contact the publisher for Library and Archives Canada catalogue information.

ALANNA RUSNAK PUBLISHING
a division of Chicken House Press
chickenhousepress.ca

It was a dark and stormy winter's night at the vet clinic.

The colourful Christmas lights danced over Mozart as he fell asleep under the tree.

CRASH!

BANG!

A noise startled Mozart awake.

"What was that?"

Mozart wondered.

"I think it came from outside."

Mozart ran to the door.

As he looked out
into the storm, a
figure appeared.

Could it be?

There's no way!

It looked like one of Santa's reindeer!

"Hello, I'm Comet,"
the reindeer said.

"I injured myself while flying so I was
sent here to get bandaged up.
Could you please help me?"

Mozart hesitated.

"I have never done that before..." he said.
"But I have seen the vet do it, so I could try."

Mozart brought Comet back into the treatment room.

THINK, THINK , THINK...

"What did they do when Hank came in with his cut?" Mozart thought to himself.

CLEAN!

They cleaned his cut!

Mozart scurried into the cupboard to find everything he needed. Then he cleaned up Comet's wound.

After some clipping, scrubbing, and
rinsing the cleaning was complete.
Comet was ready for the next step.

THINK, THINK, THINK...

"What did they do next after they cleaned Oskar's wound?" Mozart thought to himself.

COVER IT!

They covered his wound
with an ointment and pad!

Mozart scurried into the cupboard to find everything he needed to cover Comet's wound.

After some ointment and a pad,
the covering was complete.

Comet was ready
for the next step.

THINK, THINK , THINK...

"What did they do next after covering Griffin's wound?"
Mozart thought to himself.

WRAP IT!

They wrapped up
Griffin's wound!

Mozart scurried into the cupboard to find everything he needed to wrap Comet's wound.

After some tugging, pulling, and cutting
the wrapping was complete.

Comet was ready to fly again!

Mozart walked
Comet back outside.

"Thank you, Mozart!" Comet exclaimed.
"You made my leg feel much better!
I think I am ready to catch up with the team again."
And with a jingle from his bell, Comet started to fly.

"Thank you for letting me help you!" Mozart hollered
as he watched Comet fly off into the distance.

As Mozart got ready to sleep again, he started to feel a warmth down deep inside. A warmth not even the best cuddles or pets could give. It felt good helping Comet.

Maybe this is what giving is supposed to look like. Helping others.

Devotional:

Mozart was woken up late at night by a stranger asking for help at the vet clinic. Mozart had never cleaned, covered, and wrapped a wound before. He could have easily told Comet, 'No, I cannot help you,' and gone back to sleep, but instead Mozart decided to give Comet his time and care to help him out.

During the joyous Christmas season, we hear the saying 'giving is better than receiving.' Why is that?

Why would Mozart feel so good after caring for Comet?

Why do we tend to feel happier when we give something to someone else? Why is it good to give?

Luke 6:38 says, 'Give, and it will be given to you. Good measure, pressed down, shaken together, running over, will be put into your lap. For with the measure you use it will be measured back to you.'

God actually calls us to give. He wants us to help those around us whether we are friends, family, or even strangers.

When we give gifts, our time, or our care to other people around us, we are allowing God to bless others through us!

God has filled you with love, talents, time, and much more, but He doesn't want you to hold onto those gifts for yourself. Instead, He wants you to give them to others. When we give to others, we are obeying God's Word, honouring God by helping people, inspiring those around us and thinking of ourselves less while thinking about others more. We are representing what God has done for us.

John 3:16 says, 'For God so loved the world that He gave His one and only Son, that whoever believes in Him should not die but have everlasting life.'

What can you give to others this Christmas season?

Mozart the Clinic Cat

Mozart the Clinic Cat

Look for the other books in this series

NO PLACE TO SLEEP

THE LOST BUNNY

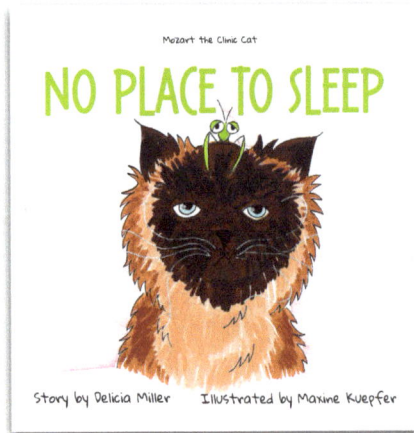

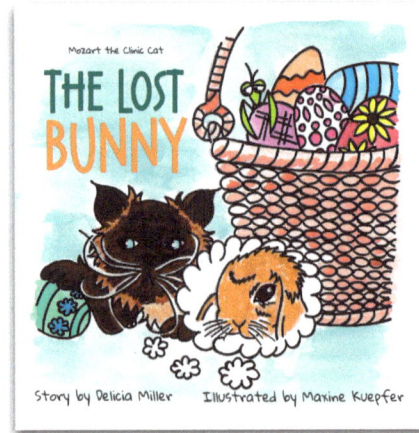

www.ingramcontent.com/pod-product-compliance
Lightning Source LLC
Chambersburg PA
CBHW042107040426

42448CB00002B/173

Mozart the Clinic Cat

A surprise guest shows up
at the clinic, and he is hurt!
Will Mozart be able to remember
all the steps the vet uses
so he can help his new friend?

Delicia Miller resides in Durham, Ontario with her husband, children, and their cat 'Nala'. Delicia works as a Children's Pastor at Crossroads Life Church and formerly worked as a Registered Veterinary Technician getting to snuggle Mozart at Laurelwood Veterinary Hospital in Waterloo, Ontario.

Maxine Kuepfer resides in Milverton, Ontario with her 11 year old lop-eared rabbit, Dudley. She studied at University of Guelph and graduated an honours program in Bachelor of Arts - Major Studio Art.

Mozart is a curious, naive Himalayan who loves to cuddle but only on his own terms. Mozart was adopted by the amazing staff at Laurelwood Veterinary Hospital where he makes sure everyone feels welcome while keeping the staff on their toes.

Juvenile Fiction | $12.99 CAN

ISBN 9781990336591

ALANNA RUSNAK PUBLISHING
alannarusnakpublishing.com

90000

9 781990 336591